EAT YOUR SPINACH

EAT YOUR SPINACH

Spend Less and Invest More

(And How To Do It)

John Gordon and Richard Howard

Library of Congress Control Number: 2006904994

ISBN: 1-4751-8638-X
ISBN-13: 9781475186383

Contents

It is not wealth one asks for, but just enough to preserve one's dignity, to work unhampered, to be generous, frank, and independent.

—William Somerset Maugham,
Of Human Bondage (1915)

ACKNOWLEDGEMENTS

Karen Brockney has contributed computer assistance and insights. Helka Gordon has been an effective reviewer. In addition, they have stayed married to us. We thank them.

ACKNOWLEDGMENT

CHAPTER 1

The Case for Controlled Frugality

A World of Plenty

In the United States, and probably in most cities around the world, one routinely sees young people decked out with a cell phone, an iPOD, one-hundred-dollar jeans, and two-hundred-dollar shoes while they shop vigorously for more clothes, toys, and exotic food and drink. Often they enjoy their own bedroom and bathroom in a large house, are driven to the mall in a shiny SUV, watch TV on huge screens, and surf the Internet on their spiffy PC. In one way this is marvelous. Never have the young, even the offspring of the affluent in rich countries, had so much disposable cash and ready comfort. Self-expression, fun, and the ability to attract friends are especially important to young people, and the consumer society is especially good at giving the youth market what it wants. We think it is a good idea to have fun while young, and as far as we can remember, we did our best to do so in that far-off time when we were in that retrospectively delightful state. We think it is commendable that the advanced economies of the "developed" world can produce the money and the avalanche of goods that make this state of affairs possible. We think it is great that young people are taking advantage of it and having a good time. We are not related to the Grinch, really.

A World of Potential Hurt

But we are worried. We think it may be that today's youth think that they will find themselves in their parents' and grandparents' environment when they reach retirement age. And many parents and even grandparents continue to spend as if there is no tomorrow. We, the authors, don't remember thinking anything at all about old age until we were well into our third decade, unless it was to feel fleeting pity for duffers over thirty. But we were part of the "lucky generation." Not only did our draft ages fall between Korea and Viet Nam, many of us didn't have to worry much about later because of the pension and Social Security policies then in place and virtually forced on us. In fact, the world is changing rapidly around today's youth, and in many ways, it is changing so that things will be much harder when they reach "retirement age" or when a recession/depression finds them in a low-paying job or none at all. Even those in or near middle age may fall into the trap of seeing things as they were, not as they will become.

Increasingly, unless people begin to save and invest as early in life as possible, they risk facing an especially bleak later life. In the United States, the social safety net is eroding. "Defined benefit" pension plans (those which promise a given, often generous, guaranteed amount on retirement) are disappearing rapidly. In the best instance, they are being replaced with "defined contribution" plans (those which promise only income from the money contributed by and for the individual over their working lifetime, but not a definite amount). Most often, for new ventures and "restructured" companies, pensions are being replaced with various government-blessed savings vehicles, such as the 401(k).

These promise long-term tax benefits, but are sharply limited in the amount of money that can be contributed to them annually. An Associated Press article by Brian Bergstein suggests that IBM's retreat from its fiscally healthy defined benefit plan will be a wake-up call because it both illustrates the demise of traditional pensions and focuses on the 401K as an alternative. This has experts worried as to whether the 401K will be adequate to provide for retirement in its current form, and as we explain below, we are sure it will not be adequate for most (*The Oregonian*, January 7, 2006).

Social Security, the perennial "third rail" of American politics, has apparently lost its politically lethal charge, and schemes to change (many would say *weaken* or *eliminate*) it are proliferating. To take undue comfort from the fact that the Bush administration has backed away from its proposed changes is to underestimate the tenacity of politicians and to ignore the dire straights into which the federal budget is plunging and the demographics of the future.

Health care costs are rising more rapidly than general inflation, and the endless supply of new miracle drugs and treatments are ever more expensive. Partly because of these drugs and treatments, people are living longer and requiring ever more of them. This longer life often includes long periods of expensive nursing care, which were rare only twenty years ago.

In the workplace, the lifetime job has become the exception rather than the rule; self-employment is on the rise. On the whole, we think this is a good thing. Self-reliance and risk taking are exhilarating. They lead to thought, effort, commitment, and achievement. But they also provide a less sure, if often ultimately larger, income stream than the "steady job" of yesteryear. This means that individuals will need to provide, through savings and investment, for periods of low or no current income.

Finally, as China and India transform into world-class economies, there is no reason to believe that the United States and other G8 countries will maintain their income edge. It may be that the rising tide of democracy and market capitalism will truly lift all boats. In fact, this is highly likely. But it is also likely that there will be a redistribution of wealth along with trade and productivity so that the relative affluence of the citizens of the G8 countries appears, and is, less. Therefore, just as poverty is often recognized in the comparison with others and not as an absolute, the amount of money one needs to feel included in the "good life" may greatly increase over the life of those now in their teens, twenties, and thirties. So far we have systematically underestimated the rate of growth and change in the BRIC countries (Brazil, Russia, India, and China). Together they contain well over half of the world's population and resources. To expect them permanently to be denied our standard of living is simpleminded.

All the above reckon without calamity. Worldwide depression, Carter-scale inflation, pestilence, bad weather, earthquakes, volcanoes, and war often have ruined the prospects of millions. Except for the first two, wealth is not a certain shield from their effects. But sometimes it is. Fair or not, people with money tended to get out of Nazi Germany easier than poor people. The affluent die at lower rates than the poor in most epidemics of most diseases. It is easier to rebuild your house and life after a hurricane if you have some money. So a prudent person is financially responsible because there are some events that are relatively predictable (old age, illness, retirement) and because some are not. We are also capable of precipitating calamity ourselves, for example, through government policies. Paul Volcker, former chairman of the Federal Reserve Board, said in late 2005: "I don't know of any country that has managed to consume and invest 6 percent more than it produces for long. I don't know whether change will come with a bang or a whimper, whether sooner or later. But as things stand, it is more likely than not that it will be financial crises rather than policy foresight that will force the change."

For a reasonably apocalyptic but well-reasoned and immensely detailed view of the financial future of those who are now young Americans, you should read, without delay, *The Coming Generational Storm: What You Need to Know About America's Economic Future* by Lawrence J. Kotlikoff and Scott Burns. If you accept their detailed analysis and logic, there is not a moment to lose to begin to prepare for your far financial future.

You Will Need a Large Pile of Money

Here is a brief example to illustrate the need for people from twenty through forty to save and invest now. Suppose that after you include your Social Security and pension income (if you're fortunate enough to get a pension), you need an additional $20,000 for the first year of your retirement. This $20,000 will come out of your own retirement savings. And further assume that each year after your expenses increase because of inflation. So the $20,000 requirement gets larger every year. Also, assume you will live for thirty years after you retire at sixty-five. Finally, if you assume an average inflation rate of 4 percent and an average rate of return of 6 percent on your investment during retirement, you will need $436,000 at the start of your retirement. Given that all the assumptions hold, you will have enough money to last thirty years.

Suppose your goal is to have $500,000 at the start of your retirement. So how do you get that amount of money? One way is to start investing at the earliest possible age. For example, if you start to invest thirty years before you retire and receive an average return of 6 percent on your investments, you need to invest $498 each month for thirty years, a total of $179,191. But if you wait until ten years before your retirement, you must invest $3,051 each month or a total of $366,123. The conclusion is obvious; start saving and investing at the earliest possible age.

People who make systematic investments many years before they retire have time on their side to allow their investments to grow to very large amounts. But people who wait to invest until a few years before retirement have to play catch-up and must invest very large amounts of money during their final years at work.

What does this simple example teach? You need a **very large pile of money** for retirement, and you should start saving and investing **many years before you retire.**

Eat Your Spinach
In the following chapters, we contrast what we think prudent fiscal behavior is with that we think isn't. We base our arguments on facts and observations of two kinds: data available in the cited sources, and our experience and that of our acquaintances. The moral is simple. More responsible fiscal behavior early will result in a better life later, and it can be achieved while still enjoying life. At the extreme, nobody we know of ever has died from eating

spinach (although Popeye may have married Olive Oil, we don't know). But if you don't eat your financial spinach young, you run the risk of living on real spinach and little else later.

We think even those who are in or near retirement can benefit from reading this book, but it is especially aimed at what we call "the young." We define "young" as anyone with a potential twenty-year investment life ahead of them. Since many of us will continue earning until we are seventy or older, this includes everyone up to at least the age of fifty.

CHAPTER 2

The Soup You Are In:
The Scope of the Problem

In this chapter, we make the quantitative case that unbridled consumerism and poor saving habits (arising from reliance on a future bull market, house-value increase, government-sponsored savings plans, low interest rates, easy borrowing, or working longer) ensure that you face a risk-laden and insecure financial future.

Unchecked consumerism seems to lead to larger things. In the United States, average house size, automobile weight, and indeed, human weight (for young and old) have increased rapidly in the recent past. Aside from the minor logic that fat people may need bigger houses and cars, this trend probably is best explained by a strong general desire to spend rather than save. Indeed, in 2005 the aggregate American savings rate turned negative. This may be because the bull stock market that ran from 1982 to 2000 has given people a sense of financial security and the hope of some similar wealth-creating market run in their future. It may also have some elements of "live as though there is no tomorrow, because there may not be one" left over from the cold war and buttressed by apocalyptic visions of the future from environmentalists and social critics.

As house prices continue to rise in most markets, people may look at their paper gains in real estate and feel wealthy enough so that they don't need to save for a rainy day or retirement. Then again, many may feel that if they make the maximum contribution to their IRA or other tax-sheltered saving plans, they have no further need to save. Certainly low mortgage interest rates, coupled with "creative" adjustable rate and interest-only mortgages, have fueled home buying and prices. Certainly the availability of easy (but far from cheap) credit through the use of a gaudy array of credit cards has contributed to a feeling of affluence on the part of those who use them. Finally, longer life spans have made it easy to say, when you are thirty, forty, or even fifty, that you will just continue to work until you are seventy or seventy-five or even longer (like the former Federal Reserve chairman, Alan Greenspan), and thus, there is no need to save, at least as much, for retirement. At the same time, underfunding of pensions is rapidly increasing. Companies with underfunded pension plans reported a record shortfall of $353.7 billion in their 2005 filings with the Pension Benefit Guaranty Corporation (PBGC). That is up considerably from the $279.0 billion reported a year earlier. The total increase in underfunding is $74.7 billion, or 27 percent, in a single year. Clearly, just because you are promised a pension doesn't mean you will ever get one, or at least the one you thought you would.

Bull Market Bull

Even if you are under thirty, there may not be another bull market to equal that of the '80s and '90s in your lifetime. If you invested in 1929 in a market index fund (which didn't exist then), you would first have seen a profit in 1954, twenty-five years later. Twenty years is at least half of the average working lifetime. Although it is true that if all of the market's twentieth- and twenty-first-century gains are considered, stocks are a better investment than bonds or real estate, the stock market can go a long time with negligible returns.

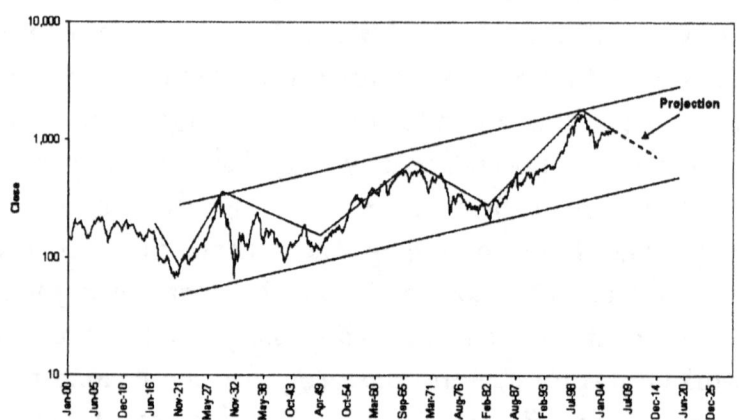

Whether you have a chance to benefit from a bull market thus depends on over how long a time you invest, and when your investment life falls in relation to market gains. Counting on a future bull market to ensure your financial future is an extreme form of gambling.

Your Home Is Your Castle, Not a Retirement Plan
House prices have had two periods of rapid increase since WWII.

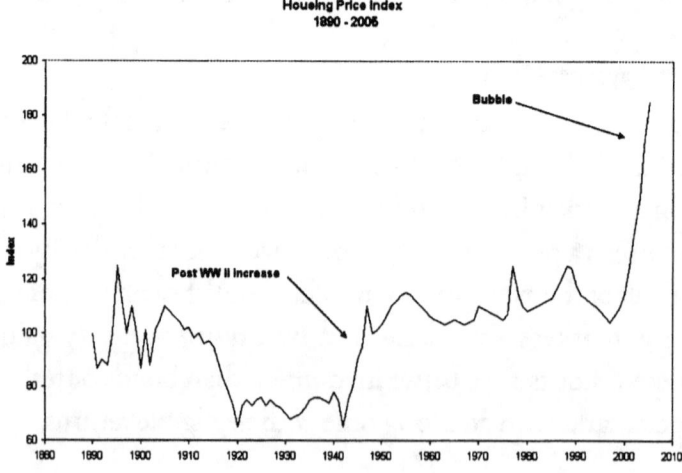

The first one followed the war when the veterans came home. The second, now, has coincided with low mortgage rates and an attractiveness of real estate as an investment in comparison to the stock market decline of 2000-2002. The current boom shows signs of leveling off in some markets, and is predicted to flatten entirely by some savvy commentators and economists. Nevertheless, owning a home, particularly owning a home free of debt, can be an important ingredient in a retirement plan. But home ownership is not a retirement plan by itself. First, home equity is useable to purchase groceries or other retirement needs only if it is somehow rendered into cash. To do this, with a true net gain, you need to sell the house you have and buy something cheaper, presumably smaller or in a different location. Let's say, by the age of sixty-five, you own, free and clear, a house of average (for the U.S.) price, worth $270,000. That is a lot of money, for sure. But can you live the rest of your life on it? Well, let's say you can buy a house adequate to your needs for half that, a reasonably optimistic assumption, and you do so. Now, you have $135,000 left to live on. If you have no moving expenses or other costs (highly unlikely), you can probably count on spending 4 percent of $135,000 annually for the rest of your life. Can you live on $5,400 per year? Maybe, if you have Social Security as well. But you are now in a likely much smaller house in a less desirable location, and living on a shoestring budget. That doesn't sound like the golden years to us.

Or you can borrow against your house, and even do a "reverse mortgage" in which the holder of your debt pays you a regular sum. Sound good? Think about this. First, you probably worked hard to pay off your mortgage to shed the feeling of being indebted to an at best uncaring stranger, and to feel that you had, at least, a secure place to live. So, when you reborrow, you lose that feeling and protection, at a time in your life when other insecurities (health, work) increase. The "reverse mortgage" simply means that you sell your house slowly back to the bank. But the bank wants to be repaid for their loan rather than taking the house. So, the house must be sold when you move or die. If this wasn't better for the bank than for you, they wouldn't do it. However, here is what a couple, aged sixty-six and sixty-five, might get for "reverse mortgaging" the $270,000 house above: either a single lump-sum advance or a credit line of $150,930. Or you can have a monthly advance of $894 as long as you live in your home ($10,728 per year). This is better, on its face, than the $135,000 above, and you stay in your house. But you again have a mortgage, with many restrictions on what you can do with "your" house. If you default on any of them, the bank can demand immediate payment up to the full market value of your house. The American Association of Retired Persons (AARP) says, "Because of the complex issues involved in reverse mortgages, AARP recommends that you read all the articles on this topic on this site (www.rmaarp.com) before requesting counseling or making any decisions." We second that, and submit that for most people, this is a partial and needlessly risky solution to retirement income.

401(k)? No Way!

As of this writing, you can put up to $14,000 a year into a tax-sheltered 401(k) account, through your employer, to accumulate tax free to be taken out without penalty (but with income tax) after you are 59 ½. If your income was large enough to allow and support that amount, and if you did it for a thirty-year working life, you would have invested $420,000 and built a considerable nest egg calculated at a midrange rate of return.

Possible 401(k) Accumulations	
Annual Return	Dollars Accumulated
4%	$816,597
6%	$1,173,223
8%	$1,712,842

The problem is that most cannot or do not do this. About 25 percent of Americans eligible for these plans do not use them at all. Most do not have sufficient income to make the maximum contribution. And typically, most do not start contributing until about the middle of their working life, either because they prefer to consume, or because their employer doesn't offer them a plan.

The Roth 401(k) is built with after-tax contributions, but income in the account accumulates tax free and no tax is owed when the money is withdrawn after you are 59 ½ years old.

Employees that do have them are not saving much money in their 401(k) retirement accounts. According to EBRI Issue Brief No. 272, a report based on retirement data maintained by the Employee Benefit Research Institute (ERBI) and the Investment Company Institute (ICI), the average account balance was $51,569 as of the end of 2003. For all participants about 67 percent of their assets were invested in stocks through equity and balanced mutual funds and company stock.

Account balances tended to increase with age and the number of years over which people had invested. The largest average balance was $178,181 for people in their sixties who had contributed for more than thirty years. That is less than one-half of what it would take to sustain a $20,000 pretax retirement income at a withdrawal rate of 4 percent per year. About 18 percent of plan participants had outstanding loans, and the average loan balance was $6,839. So the average 401(k) account balance minus loans was $44,730. The first lesson here is to use your 401k, Roth and conventional IRA to the maximum to gain the benefit to tax-sheltered compounding (Appendix E). Second, unless you are far above average in income and grit when it comes to saving, your 401(k) will not support an adequate retirement income by itself.

The Easy Credit Trap

Credit cards are wonderful. They are portable, relatively safe compared to cash, provide ancillary benefits (airline miles, rebates), and provide a convenient record of purchases, making budget reconciliation easy, among other things. They make life easier in many ways. Unfortunately, they make borrowing money easier. Borrowing through a credit card has some advantages—being quick, free of voluminous loan applications, and unsecured (they can't easily take your house if you default, for example). But this very convenience is a moral hazard. It tempts you to borrow more than you should and at truly frightening interest rates. The LowCard$.com Web site, for example, listed the ten best credit card APR rates on October 14, 2005, as 10.74, 10.49, 9.99 (three), 11.24, 6.99, 8.5, 11.74, and 10.24. The card listed at 6.99 has exceptionally stringent access and repayment requirements. All but two are listed as variable rates, meaning they can go up as well as down. On the same day, Bankrate.com listed the overnight average rates on certificates of deposit (CD) as 3.22 percent for a six-month, 3.78 for a one-year, and 4.15 for a five-year CD. The top three one-year CD rates listed on the site for the same day were 4.50, 4.50, and 4.41. These latter three had minimum investment requirements of $5,000, $10,000, and $10,000, respectively. Basically, this means that for almost everyone, paying off credit card debt (and then staying out of it) is better than putting money in the bank. The long-term return on the stock market is said to be somewhere in the 6 to 10 percent range, and is probably closer to the smaller figure.

According to a Reuters story, dated October 12, 2005, a survey by DEMOS and the Center for Responsible Lending showed that 33 percent of the 1,150 low- and middle-income families included in the study used credit card debt to fund daily living expenses, including groceries and utilities. Their average debt was $8,650. Thus, even if they were paying the "lowest" rates above, they spend at least $800 a year on credit debt service. That is close to the average annual light bill for a small home. The "fine print" on credit card agreements is confusing in its detail and language, and federal regulation of credit card companies is not "meaningful," according to the groups who did the survey.

Paying exorbitant credit card interest is the fierce enemy of saving, particularly by the young. Eat your spinach and cut it out.

Make "Work Longer" a Choice, Not a Burden

Although we think it is a good idea to keep working, by the time you are sixty-five or so, you will also probably want a choice, or a change. Illness or infirmity often makes work less fun, or even impossible, in our later years. Even while in good health, we have noticed, in ourselves and our friends, that perceptions about work can change very rapidly as we progress into our sixties. Hobbies, family, and travel become more important as we see time getting shorter. A form of the "Wager of Pascal" seems to apply here. He said, in essence, "If you bet there is a god and there isn't, you have lost nothing. If you bet there isn't a god and there turns out to be one, you could be in real trouble." Similarly, if you prepare for old age by becoming financially independent, there is nothing to stop you from continuing to work until you drop. But if you don't prepare, you could be bagging groceries or greeting shoppers at Wal-Mart when you drop.

We hope you are convinced that there is at least a case for consuming less now to assure a brighter future. But we are eager to avoid the mistake people often make when "advising" the very young. Parents tend to say, "Don't fall out of that tree!" We don't recall ever wanting to fall out of a tree, and we suppose not many children do now. They are interested in how not to fall out of the tree, and that is what the rest of this book is about: how to stay in and climb further upward in life's financial tree.

CHAPTER 3

Find Your Way to Wealth:
A Simple Map for Success

In our earlier book *Buy on the Upside: Outsider Advice and Encouragement for the Stock Investor* and our companion Web site *buyupside.com*, we point out that successful stock investing takes commitment and hard work. There are many pitfalls to be avoided; buying overpriced "miracle" stocks, uncritical acceptance of the avalanche of advice from the "Wall Street Buy Machine," trading too much, trading too little, and putting too many eggs in a single basket, to name a few. But we want to assure you that successful investing is neither wholly a matter of luck nor a complicated science. In this chapter we give an overview of the relatively simple set of steps that will lead to enjoyment of your well-earned wealth. In subsequent chapters, we will detail each step for you and tell you what to watch out for.

Most of what we stay applies to other forms of investment such as bonds or rental real estate. Although this book is focused on stocks, we think a balanced investment picture for most people will include bonds (often referred to as "fixed income" securities or "debt") and real estate, as well as stocks. Bonds, stocks, and real estate are now available to the beginning investor through highly liquid and diversified trading vehicles such as stock mutual funds, bond funds, index and exchange-traded funds (ETFs), and real estate investment trusts (REITs). Typically and prudently, the balance of an investor's portfolio shifts toward fixed income with advancing age. The older you are, the less time you have to benefit from the long-term upward trend of the stock and real estate markets, and typically, the more you desire, the lower risk profile of highly-rated bonds. However, we believe every portfolio should include some proportion of stocks since they are the most likely to keep up with inflation and, thus, to preserve the purchasing power of the income from your suite of investments.

If you are twenty and struggling to pay tuition or the rent, this all may seem pretty esoteric. "Suite of investments" indeed. What on earth are we talking about? Let's look at the map components.

Save and Invest Now

The first stop on the map says "save and invest now." The overall message is that you should cut your expenses enough to save at least some money every month, no matter what your income, and you start doing it now. The smaller your income, the harder this is, although there are many, many people with average or even princely incomes who save little or nothing, and there are many people on a modest budget who save regularly and in the course of time become "comfortable" or even "well-off." Two equations have been true for the ages:

> expenditures greater than income=misery
> income greater than expenditures=peace of mind.

Note the word *budget*. The absolutely necessary first step is knowledge. Construct a budget that plans your expenditures and tracks your actual performance. Then make sure that you "pay yourself first"—that is, save before you spend—and do it automatically through bank account transfers to savings or an investment account. Make sure you are taking advantage of any tax-sheltered opportunities to save and make sure that any potential employer contributions are captured.

Continually look for ways to cut expenses and shift consumption to saving. Does this mean holes in your shirt or dress and thin gruel for dinner? Not unless you enjoy thin gruel. Usually it means things like not paying for designer labels, not eating high cost (low-nutrition food that is bad for you anyway), and cultivating the habit of taking pleasure from less expensive rather than more expensive things. Just as the Wall Street Buy Machine tells you that buying any stock is always a good idea, the Main Street Buy Machine tells you that every new fashion, label, and gadget must be bought and exhibited. Ostentation, showing off how much you can spend by displaying expensive clothes and toys, is one of the oldest human traits. Thorstein Veblen, in his economic classic "Theory of the Leisure Class," recounts the tale of the prince who allowed himself to be toasted rather than move away from the fire, to avoid giving the impression that he couldn't afford lackeys to carry him. That may be extreme, but if conspicuous consumption keeps you from saving, particularly early in your life, you will surely be financial toast later.

Accumulate Wealth the Easy Way

Once you have the structure (budget, accounts) and habit of saving, you have reached the second and lifelong stop on the map: "accumulate wealth." If you buy and hold stocks with increasing dividends, reinvest the dividends to accumulate more stock. You will be surprised at how fast shares and value accumulate. Similarly, if you buy only low-fee, exchange-traded or index mutual funds, your wealth will build much faster, surprisingly so, than if you buy high-fee "managed" funds.

We advocate simplicity in investing. One such investment plan is to keep half your money in certificates of deposit and invest half in the Standard & Poors 500 Index, which tracks the five hundred largest companies in the United States. The Vanguard 500 Index (VFINX), Fidelity Spartan 500 Index Investor (FSMKX), and SPDRs (SPY) are appropriate choices to track the S&P 500. Held over the long term, with income reinvested, these investments should ensure that you build a nest egg with low expense and little trouble. With these simple plans, there is no need to bother learning all about stocks, bonds, and other types of investments useless you find them interesting.

Ben Stein, on his Web site, offers an extremely simple recipe for those who value simplicity. Each month invest a fixed amount equally into two exchange-traded funds (ETFs). One, with the ticker symbol RWR, holds the Wilshire REIT (real estate investment trust) Index, and the other, iShares Dow Jones Select Dividend Index (DVY), holds the top fifty dividend-paying stocks. Here you profit from rising real estate values as well as corporate profits of some of the largest companies in the United States.

If you work for a company, particularly one you like, it is tempting to load your 401(k) or your other investment accounts with its stock. Don't. One word is sufficient to convey this warning: Enron. Similarly, avoid high-fee hedge funds and most annuities. Their charges are almost always out of line with their performance.

Learn What Kind of Investor You Are

Doing the above will, by itself, make you "comfortable" or "well-off" or even "rich" if you do them long and diligently enough (a recent definition of "rich" is no debt, a place in the city, a place in the country, and a $5 million net worth). But if you want to become an aggressive investor (one who buys and sells more frequently than the investor described above), keep three cardinal rules in mind. First, don't pay too much. Burt Malkiel, the "intellectual father of index funds," says in his investment books that "too much" is any stock priced much above the average market price to earnings ratio. Second, buy when a stock or the market is "on the upside," that is, increasing in value. Third, sell stocks when they have either appreciated significantly or decreased substantially (say 10 percent) below their purchase price for reasons other than general market movement. This is the old gambler's adage, "cut your losses but let your winnings run," with the proviso to take profits at prudent times so that winnings don't evaporate. It is good to have numerical targets since it is very difficult to identify market or individual stock tops and bottoms. We advocate keeping a substantial portion of your total investment funds in cash, say 15 to 20 percent, to be able to take advantage of buying opportunities. Although many financial advisers tout being "fully invested," having plenty of cash creates opportunities for the aggressive investor and bolsters peace of mind besides.

The Payoff

The final stop on the map is financial security. You have created or are preparing for a comfortable retirement. More importantly, perhaps, you have become an active leader in your personal life. Because you have taken charge of your finances, you will have greater peace of mind. Living from paycheck to paycheck is nerve-racking at best, and if the paycheck you are living toward disappears, it is downright disastrous and destructive of the self-confidence that enables success in most of life's pursuits. Much of the enjoyment of wealth comes from contemplating the future choices and opportunities it confers. Thus, you can think about comfortable retirement and enjoy the thoughts long before you retire. You can plan for a trip, or a boat, or a vacation home, and enjoy the planning, knowing that you are on a path that will afford them. Just as much happiness comes from things remembered; much can also come from things contemplated when they are based on realistic expectations. You can and will enjoy wealth even as you build it.

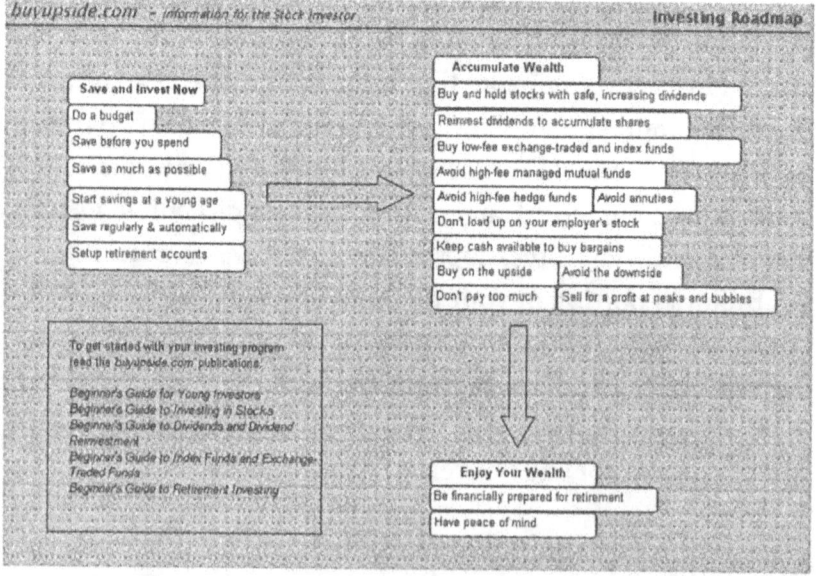

Figure 1. A simple map for financial success

Those are the locations on the map to financial security: save, invest, and enjoy. If you learn them, and learn to like them, your whole life will be better. We guarantee it.

CHAPTER 4

Act or Die: Save and Invest Now

The chapter title is a little dire. But fear or despair caused by financial uncertainty causes stress, and stress is an enemy of wellness, so perhaps it is not as far fetched as it at first seems. In any event, the "save and invest now" maxim has not been heeded by many contemporary Americans. If you act on it, you will set yourself apart from the herd, and be happier. Here is how.

Do a Budget

The first step toward building a long-term savings and investing program is to prepare a budget that spells out how you spend your money. Work out a budget and stick to it so you can pay your bills and save for your long-term financial needs.

First, write down all your expenses such as rent or mortgage payment, utilities, insurance, car payment, car expenses, food, clothes, entertainment, vacations, presents, furnishings, medical, taxes, and more. Budgets should be detailed up to the point at which the detail keeps you from actually using one. Then prioritize the items putting the most important expenses first. Be sure to include savings at the top of the list of expenses. Save at least 10 percent of your total before tax income. If you can save more, do so. If you can't save 10 percent, then save as much as you can, but make sure you are stretching to do it.

If your income does not cover your expenses, reduce expenses that are not absolutely necessary. You can cut back on gifts, vacations, entertainment, furnishings, and purchases of more "stuff." Most of us already have more things than any realistic assessment of true need would dictate. Sometimes it helps to inventory the things you have and consider how you could get more pleasure or utility out of each item. For example, most of us spend more on cars than we actually need to. Can you take public transportation to work and use part of the saved gas and wear and tear on your car for a weekend trip? Or how about food? Prepared food (especially "fast food") costs far more per unit of nutrition than basic ingredients that you prepare yourself. Cooking can be fun and is a good way to attract and impress friends, and is likely to be better for you than restaurant or "carryout" food. If you are in a position to buy a house, consider making a down payment on something less expensive than the banker says you can afford, and put or keep this "extra" money in savings or to invest. Although houses can be a very good investment, they are usually too large a portion of your portfolio for good diversification, and the bigger they are, the more they preclude other investments.

As you financial situation changes, adjust your budget accordingly. If you are fortunate and earn more money, increase your savings rather than spending.

Save Before You Spend

Why is saving a dollar important? Every dollar that you save now can be invested and then be available to you in the future. For example, one dollar invested at six percent for thirty years results in $5.74. So for every $1,000 you save and invest now, you will have $5,740 in thirty years. In forty years you will have $10,290, and in fifty years $18,420. That's real money!

Here are some savings tips that will benefit you and your wallet:

- Make savings your number 1 priority. After you pay the essential bills like mortgage or rent, utilities, car payment, taxes, and the like, pay yourself by adding money to your savings account.
- Make extra payments on your mortgage. Just a few more dollars each month will reduce your principal and reduce your number of mortgage payments. If you can double your principal payment (relatively easy when the principal is small), you will greatly reduce the interest you pay over the life of the mortgage.
- If you refinance or pay off any loans, invest the money (at least the interest) you save on your payments rather than spend it.
- Downsize your wants and needs. Do you really need the largest SUV on the market? Wouldn't a midsize model do (consider a hybrid SUV if you must have one; some states offer handsome tax credits for hybrids)? Will the latest HDTV really make you happy? If you must own it, wait a year or so until it comes down in price. Is a 4,000-square-foot house necessary? Wouldn't a 2,500-square-foot model do? That is twice as much space as the average American family had twenty years ago. The money saved by downsizing could fund a financially carefree retirement without cramping your lifestyle.
- Cut back on those frequent seemingly "small" expenses, which add up quickly to a surprising total. For example,

eating lunch out and eating snacks from vending machines cost real money.

- Share your kids' toys with your neighbors. Does every family in the neighborhood need a basketball hoop in their driveway?
- If you smoke, stop. You will save a small fortune, and you might save your life as well. A pack-per-day smoker spends $1,000 to $1,500 each year. That's enough money, if invested each year, to fund a modest retirement account all by itself.
- Save money for a purchase and then pay cash instead of using credit cards. You will reduce your impulse buying and be free of outrageous interest payments.
- Teach your children the value of a dollar. Maybe they will be content with low-cost sneakers and affordable jeans. Put away the money saved for their college education.
- Does junior really need a cell phone? Those monthly cell charges, if invested instead, would make a considerable nest egg over time.

Save As Much As You Can

The key to accumulating money is a systematic savings and investing program. Putting aside money every paycheck and then investing it wisely ensures that you will build a sizable pile of money over time.

Suppose you make $50,000 a year and you save 5 percent of your gross salary each year. Further assume that your salary increases three percent each year.

The following table shows how much money you would accumulate given an annual return on your savings of 6 percent or 8 percent.

Accumulated Money at a 5 Percent Savings Rate		
Years	6% Return	8% Return
10	$37,244	$40,750
20	$116,752	$142,742
30	$276,352	$381,770
40	$585,307	$923,124
50	$1,169,687	$2,125,885
Note: If you saved 10 percent, the dollar amounts would double.		

This simple example shows the power of saving and investing for many years. If you have the discipline to stick to a systematic savings and investing program, then time will ensure that you will accumulate lots of money. And if you are a savvy investor and can achieve higher returns on your investments, you can significantly increase your total accumulation.

Many people begin serious investing in the stock market when they reach their forties and fifties. With retirement coming in a few years, they attempt to play catch-up and hope for large returns to fund their retirement nest egg. To this end more than half the families in the United States are invested in the stock market. Why do they choose to own stocks? Because for the last one hundred years, the returns from the stock market have outpaced other popular kinds of investments like bonds and certificates of deposits.

But the stock market doesn't go up every year. In fact, there have been periods when the stock market went down for several years or was flat for many years. If you are middle-aged and happen to invest during an off period, you may not accumulate enough money in your stock portfolio to fund your retirement. However, if you invest at a very young age and hold your investments for a long time, say forty or fifty years, you can counteract the ups and downs of the market and you will have a very good chance of making lots of money. The secret is to invest for a long time.

Start Young

The message, then, is to start investing at the earliest possible age. With a rising long-term stock market and many years of investing, you are almost certain to achieve large long-term returns. For example, $1,000 invested each year in the United States stock market from 1954 to 2003 grew to $537,493 as of June 25, 2004. So a $50,000 investment grew tenfold. This simple example shows that you don't have to be wealthy to make money in the market. You simply need a modest amount of money, discipline to invest regularly, and lots of time. Obviously, no one knows what the future will bring for the stock market, but if you assume the long-term future will be somewhat like the last fifty years, you should make lots of money investing in stocks.

Just imagine how much money you could accumulate if you started a systematic savings and investment program when you are eighteen. And then you continued the program throughout your adult life.

Teens and young adults have lots of money at their disposal. Many receive a regular allowance from their parents. Many have part-time or full-time jobs. Most kids receive money from their parents and relatives on birthdays, special religious celebrations, and holidays. Some are given money for academic and other achievements. Often, high school and college seniors receive money as a graduation present. And cash gifts are common as wedding presents.

In our affluent world teens and young adults are consumers like all of us. So they tend to spend much of the money they receive and earn. Most young people spend lots of money on clothes, food, and entertainment. Many own cars and others have expensive hobbies. Some are in college or on their own and pay rent and utilities.

Although saving money may be difficult, it's very important that young people become regular savers and investors. Because they have lots of time of their side, their investment dollars have the potential of making huge gains.

Set up Retirement Accounts and Save Automatically

The following list is your key to profitable investing for a lifetime:

1. Start a systematic savings program at the earliest age. Park your money in certificates of deposit until you start buying stocks. A good time to start is after you have the equivalent of six months' salary in the bank.
2. Begin making contributions to a Roth IRA as soon as you earn taxable income from a part-time or full-time job.
3. Own shares of the five hundred largest companies in the United States by owning the Standard & Poor's 500 stock index (S&P 500) or an even broader index through index or exchange-traded funds (ETFs).

4. Reinvest all dividends you receive.
5. Set up a systematic schedule of contributions.
6. Hold your shares until you retire.

Each of the steps is easy to understand and implement. The following discussion gives you specific recommendations and instructions how to construct your lifetime investing program.

Before you can invest your money for the long term, you must have the money to invest. Many people spend their money so quickly that they don't have any left to save and invest. You want to learn how to avoid the no-savings trap.

To save money requires that you discipline yourself to set aside some percentage of your income, allowance, and monetary gifts *before* you spend that money. As a start, think about saving at least 10 percent of your income, monetary gifts, and allowance. If you can save a higher percentage, that's even better. Remember that the more you save and invest at the earliest possible age, the more money you'll have in the future.

Follow these five simple rules to save money:

- Save first, then spend—make **savings**, not spending, your top priority.
- Save money every time you receive money—get into the savings habit; be a disciplined saver.
- Save as much as you can—even a few dollars saved is better than nothing saved.
- As your income increases, save more—save added income, don't spend it all.

- Save forever—continue to save even when you feel you have enough money. Because of inflation (rising cost of living), money doesn't go as far as you might think.

Finally, think about this idea: "Having money doesn't ensure happiness, but not having money makes happiness (and life generally) more difficult." One of the authors of this book (John Gordon) was in his mid forties before taking saving seriously. His philosophy had been "I will have a pension and Social Security when I am old; therefore, I can spend all I make now." It took a divorce and a period of ensuing relative poverty to wake him up. With good luck and considerable effort, he was able to retire ahead of schedule, but with far less put away than if he had started fifteen or twenty years earlier.

CHAPTER 5

Persevere: Accumulate Wealth

You have accomplished something few do. You have established yourself as a disciplined saver and a committed investor. Your task now is to maintain your discipline while continuing to accumulate wealth. To do this, you will need several tools. Most financial advisors recommend a "buy and hold" strategy. This isn't a panacea, and the compact phrase "buy and hold" conceals many nuances, some of them fairly nasty. But one of the positive implications is the notion of "dividend reinvestment."

Buy and Hold Stocks That Pay Safe, Increasing Dividends

Dividend reinvestment is a systematic method of accumulating shares of a stock that pays a dividend. After you purchase a stock, simply enroll in the company's dividend reinvestment plan (DRIP), and your dividends will be automatically used to purchase additional shares. Also, you may send voluntary contributions to purchase additional shares. For a mutual fund, be sure to check off the dividend reinvestment option on your application form.

Because you pay taxes on dividends, consider putting dividend reinvestment stocks in a retirement account so you can shelter the dividends from your current tax liability.

Examples of Dividend Reinvesting

This discussion includes five examples of dividend reinvestment for stocks owned by Richard Howard. Therefore, we will describe the examples in his words.

"All the data are actual numbers taken from my dividend reinvestment account statements. The DRIP summary table illustrates the results of dividend reinvesting for one mutual fund and four stocks.

Symbol	# Shares With DRIP	# Shares W/O DRIP	Price	$ Value With DRIP	$ Value W/O DRIP	% Increase Due to DRIP
VFINX	89.345	58.979	$115.82	$10,347.94	$6,830.95	51.49%
AXP	41.736	39.465	$51.43	$2,146.48	$2,029.68	5.75%
JCI	62.299	53.948	$72.88	$4,540.35	$3,931.73	15.48%
WWY	197.465	158.024	$67.68	$13,364.43	$10,695.06	24.96%
Price and number of shares as of December 28, 2005.						

As you study these examples, note how relatively modest amounts of investment dollars produced handsome returns.

Vanguard 500 Index Fund Investor Shares

I opened an Individual Retirement Account (IRA) in 1987 with the Vanguard Group and bought the Vanguard 500 Index Fund (VFINX), which is a low-fee index fund that tracks the S&P 500. The fund pays distributions in the form of dividends and capital gains.

In 1987 I invested $1,513 in eight purchases and bought 58.979 shares. On December 28, 2005, the account market value was $10,347.94. Without the reinvested distributions, the account would have been worth $6,830.95. Reinvestment of the distributions increased the number of shares by 51.49 percent, and thus the account value by 51.49 percent.

American Express

American Express (AXP) is a financial services company best known for its American Express charge card. Its current dividend yield is only 0.9 percent. I included AXP here to illustrate the negligible effect that a low-dividend yield has on share accumulation. I bought 39.465 shares AXP in 1997, and the account total was 41.367 shares at the end of 2005, only a 5.75 percent increase in seven years. You don't accumulate shares very rapidly with low-yielding stocks.

Johnson Controls

Johnson Controls (JCI) manufactures control systems and automotive parts. JCI is a growth stock with a multiyear price upside. I invested $1,000 from 1995 through 1997. I have 62.299 shares. Adjusting for the splits, the reinvested dividends have increased the share total by 15.48 percent.

Wrigley

Wrigley (WWY), the well-known maker of chewing gum, has a steady history of growing earnings and paying dividends. The current yield is 1.7 percent. Wrigley is one of my favorite companies, and I invested $2,600 from 1991 to 1996 to purchase 158.234 shares. Currently, my account has 197.465 shares, a 24.96 percent increase due to dividend reinvestment. And the $2,600 investment has grown to over $13,364.43, primarily due to price appreciation, but helped by dividend reinvestment.

Setting up Your Dividend Reinvestment Account

Here are a few ways to reinvest dividends:

- Use a full-service broker. Most brokerage firms let you reinvest dividends for the stocks you own in your account. Ask your broker for details.
- Use an Internet discount broker who offers DRIPs (both this and the full-service broker offer the advantage of having all your stocks in one place, which ensures easy record keeping and tax and estate planning). Go to BUYandHOLD or Folio*fn*.
- Buy directly from a company. Contact a company through its Web site or a service such as Computershare. Be sure to understand the fees charged by a direct stock purchase plan.
- Buy from a subscription service. See the *Moneypaper*, a monthly newsletter that offers many dividend-paying stocks.
- Buy through a bank transfer agent. For example, see the Bank of New York Web site. Type *dividend reinvestment*.

Always inquire about the fees associated with reinvesting dividends because some plans charge hefty fees. Remember that any fee, no matter the amount, reduces your profits.

Buy Low Fee Exchange-traded and Index Funds

You can buy the S&P 500 through a special type of mutual fund called an index fund, which mirrors the return of the Standard & Poor's 500 stock index. The index fund is not managed by a professional manager, so it is very inexpensive to run compared to a managed mutual fund, which requires hands-on buying and selling of stock.

A low-fee index fund that tracks the S&P 500 is the Vanguard 500 Index Trust Investor Shares (VFINX). It owns the five hundred companies that comprise the S&P 500. You can buy the Vanguard 500 Index Fund Investor Shares directly from the Vanguard Group, a leading low-cost mutual fund company.

Another way to own the S&P 500 is with an exchange-traded fund (ETF), which you may buy and sell like a stock. The exchange-traded fund that tracks the S&P 500 is called the SPY. You can purchase shares of the SPY from any brokerage firm. You will pay a small commission to buy the SPY and another small commission to sell it. But unlike a mutual fund, you will not pay any annual fees to own it in your account.

Either the Vanguard Index 500 or the SPY is appropriate for any retirement account.

All retirement accounts are subject to fees charged by the financial institution. Try to minimize these fees because they add up and will reduce your total return. Even seemingly small fees can have a significant impact on your total returns. The types of fees include: setup fee to open the account, transaction fee to buy and sell an investment, annual fee to maintain the account, inactivity fee for an account with few or no transactions, redemption fee for withdrawing money, and transfer fee to transfer your account from one institution to another. Also, many accounts have a minimum dollar amount required to open an account.

Before you open an account, take time to understand the fee schedules. Here are three low-fee financial institutions that offer the S&P 500: the Vanguard Group, Scottrade, and BUYandHOLD.

We recommend investing in the broad United States stock market as defined by the Standard & Poor's 500 stock index, as we have said above. The S&P 500 includes the five hundred largest publicly traded companies in the United States. Thus, it is a diverse mix of all types of companies like IBM, General Electric, Microsoft, and Colgate that provide goods and services to the United States and the world. With the S&P 500, you don't have to attempt to pick a few stocks that may or may not do well. You can sleep well knowing that your diversified portfolio of five hundred companies will protect you from a few bad apples. Many other broad index funds are available including those that cover medium sized and small companies.

As a shareholder of the S&P 500, you are entitled to benefit from the good fortune of these companies. As they grow their businesses and profits, their stock prices will increase, and you'll make money from this price appreciation. Some of the companies will generate excess cash and distribute it to shareholders in the form of cash dividends. You may take the dividends in cash, or you may reinvest them and buy more shares of stock. I recommend that you reinvest the dividends.

The combination of dividends and stock-price appreciation ensures that your long run returns will be greater than most other types of investments. Of course, there will be periods when the stock market is doing well and some years when it's doing poorly. But over the long run, you can expect the S&P 500 to rise in price.

The U.S. stock market includes thousands of stocks and mutual funds. With all these choices available, why do we recommend the S&P 500? My primary reason is because it is very difficult to pick stocks and mutual funds that have a better long-term performance (makes you more money) than the S&P 500. Most professionally managed mutual funds do less well than the S&P 500 in the long run. Of course, some funds do better, but it takes lots of time and study to pick the winners. The same is true with individual stocks. If you pick a winner, you can make huge amounts of money in a short time. But you can also lose a lot of money very quickly if you pick a loser.

Tax Shelter Your Gains

We recommend that you establish a Roth Individual Retirement (IRA) account. The U.S. government established the Roth IRA to encourage people to save for their long-term financial needs. The primary advantage of the Roth IRA is that you never pay any tax on gains that you achieve in the account. This tax shelter feature is a boon to investors because taxes take a big chunk of your investment returns.

You may set up a Roth IRA at any age when you begin to receive earned income from a part-time or full-time job. Earned income is money you receive in wages, tips, and salaries. Gifts and allowance money do not qualify as earned income. You can contribute $1 for each earned income up to a maximum of $14,000 for one calendar year. If you have no earned income for a year, you cannot make any contributions to your IRA for that year.

You may start to withdraw money from the Roth IRA after age 59 ½, and you'll pay absolutely no taxes on any gains you made on your investments in the account. If you withdraw money before 59 ½, you must pay substantial penalties. Remember that the Roth IRA is intended as a retirement buy-and-hold account for long-term investing. So if you need money for immediate needs like school, travel, medical expenses, etc., do not put that money in your IRA account. Once the money is in the IRA account, it should stay there until you retire.

You may set up a Roth IRA at most banks, brokerage firms, and mutual fund companies. I recommend that you select a financial institution that:

- Offers an S&P 500 index fund—some institutions do not offer the S&P 500 as an investment option.
- Charges very low fees—fees can substantially reduce your returns.
- Offers automatic investing—you may want to make automatic investments each month or another time interval.

A company that generates excess cash that it doesn't need for operations often distributes that cash to its shareholders in the form of cash dividends.

Discipline and convenience are the keys to regular savings and investing. When you have a steady stream of earned income from a part-time or full-time job, you can decide to regularly invest a fixed amount of money to your Roth IRA. For example, you could contribute $100 each month. The most convenient method to invest regularly is to set up an automatic transfer from your checking or savings account to your Roth IRA account. Most IRA accounts let you set up the transfers online. So in a few minutes, you simply specify the dollar amount of the transfer, the day of the month of the transfer, and your bank account information (routing and account numbers).

Use Dollar-cost Averaging

With automatic investing, you add new money to your IRA at regular intervals. This means that when you invest new money, you will be buying an investment different prices. When the market is down, you'll buy more shares than when the market is up. This process is called dollar-cost averaging because the cost of all your shares is the average of what you paid for each share. Some shares were cheap, and some were more expensive. Dollar-cost averaging is a simple way of systematically investing for the long term.

Typically buy-and-hold investors use dollar-cost averaging in retirement accounts and dividend reinvestment plans and fund the purchases with payroll deductions or automatic debits from a bank account. All large mutual funds and many brokerage accounts allow automatic investing.

Here is a simple example of dollar-cost averaging. Suppose you invest $100 each month to buy shares of a stock. The following table shows five monthly purchases at different prices and the resulting number of shares and their value.

Dollar-cost Averaging					
Date	Price per Share	$ Invested	# Shares Bought	Total # Shares Owned	Total $ Value
March 1	$50	$100	2.000	2.000	$100.00
April 1	$52	$100	1.923	3.923	$204.00
May 1	$58	$100	1.724	5.647	$327.54
June 1	$56	$100	1.786	7.433	$416.24
July 1	$61	$100	1.639	9.072	$553.41

After five purchases the total amount invested is $500, and you own 9.072 shares. Therefore, the average cost per share is $55.11 ($500/9.072). As of July 1, the 9.072 shares are worth $553.41.

3M (MMM) investors, who started dollar-cost averaging purchases of $100 per month in January 1976, realized a peak value of $427,658 in June 2004 for a $34,200 investment. As of February 13, 2006, the value was $359,106 for a $36,200 investment.

MMM
Dollar Value of Monthly Investments

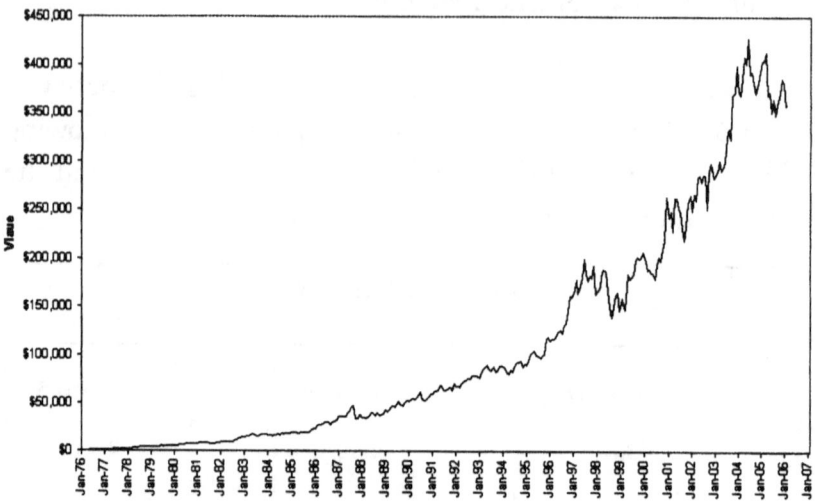

These returns resulted from a systematic long-term investment plan that coincided with an increasing stock price. Clearly, dollar-cost averaging made enormous sums of money for these 3M shareholders.

What Can Go Wrong with Your Investing Plan?

So what could go wrong with the lifetime plan of investing in stocks? The worst-case scenario would be for the U.S. economy to crumble for a long period just before or during your retirement. In this case, your portfolio would lose value when you needed to withdraw money.

If you are concerned that a prolonged downturn is coming, there are investment tactics that you could execute to protect your portfolio from serious losses. The simplest would be to sell some of your stock and keep the proceeds in cash. You probably would not make much interest from the cash but you would not lose a lot of money if stock prices were to fall.

But obviously, no one knows what economic conditions will be in fifty years. So at a young age you should be more concerned about saving and investing today rather than worrying about what could happen in fifty years.

Dollar-cost averaging (above) is a systematic investing technique used to accumulate shares of stock or a mutual fund over many months or years. You invest a specified amount of money to buy shares at a regular interval, say each month, and then you hold them for the long term.

As the stock price moves up, a specified dollar amount purchases fewer shares, but when the stock price moves down, you buy more shares. The average price per share is computed by dividing the total cost of all shares by the number of shares. Thus, you dollar-cost average and gain a degree of protection from market swings.

The best insurance against unforeseen disasters (and most are) is to stay diversified, invest regularly over time (dollar-cost averaging, DRIP), and keep a healthy cash reserve. None of these is by itself foolproof, but together they give you the best protection available.

CHAPTER 6

Celebrate: Enjoy Your Wealth All the Time

Because saving and investing require a lifelong commitment to be most effective, it is important that you take steps to stay motivated to do them both all your life. This means that you have to know what makes you want to continue saving and investing, and to make sure that you do the things that keep you on the track to wealth. As with any endeavor, self-knowledge is the key to this. For many, some combination of four things will accomplish this when tuned to your own personality and desires. The four are: (1) learn to enjoy the prospect of wealth; (2) pay yourself dividends at important milestones; (3) form a contact group for mutual encouragement; and (4) take active steps to become the "leader of your life."

Learn to enjoy the prospect of wealth
Human happiness seems often to derive from things remembered or things contemplated for the future. You can use this as a motivation to save and invest. Make conservative forecasts about where your investment plan will take you in five, ten, twenty, and thirty years. Visualize what you will be able to do as a result and imagine this in as much detail as you find interesting. Will you have enough to travel widely if that is something you value? Then think in detail about where you would go and what you would

do. Is a second home a goal for your plan? Think about where it will be and what you will do there. For most of us, it is necessary to have a good reason to defer gratification, and the more concrete and clearly seen the reason is, the easier the deferral will be.

This technique works in the short term as well. If you plan to save fifty dollars this week by taking public transportation and eating at home, calculate how much money that will be in twenty years and think about what you can do with it then. The main thing is to keep yourself and those that influence you in a positive frame of mind about saving and investing. Anything that becomes an apparently pointless chore has little chance of long-term survival.

Also, not all motivation has to be the contemplation of positive outcomes. As Samuel Johnson said, "Depend upon it, sir, when a man knows he is to be hanged in a fortnight, it concentrates his mind wonderfully." It may be possible to concentrate your mind on saving and investing by envisioning yourself bagging groceries and eating dog food at age seventy-five.

Pay yourself dividends at important milestones

Just as "all work and no play make Jack a dull boy," total austerity and lack of fun can make you a reluctant or relapsed investor. Prevent this by setting frequent saving and investment goals, and specifying what you will do to celebrate them. These celebrations should occur several times a year, and need not be (should not be, at least early on) extravagant. But they should be things you really want and enjoy and that are built into your budget. They can range from a new shirt or blouse to a trip to Europe or a NASCAR race. The main thing is that you want them, and you get them because you met a saving or investment goal. Some find it helpful to classify everything as an "input" or an "output." In this sense, saving and investment are inputs. The things you enjoy or seek are outputs.

Some lucky people can see further saving and investment as a reward (or output) in itself. If you invest the equivalent of a trip to Europe and calculate the return over five years, you may be quite surprised and pleased. In any case, it is important to see saving and investment as positive things that improve your life now and later. The "now" improvement may be at first hard to see, but once your plan is in effect, you will be surprised at how much it bolsters your self-confidence and improves your attitude toward the future.

Form a contact group for mutual encouragement

One of the most pleasant ways to enjoy the path to wealth is to find a like-minded person or persons and meet with them regularly to talk about saving and investing. Doing this takes some energy but has an array of benefits. First, since saving causes some pain and investing demands hard work, it helps to have others who understand this and will listen to your specific story in return for your listening to theirs. Also, since two or more heads are always better than one, at least in terms of the sum of information and knowledge contained, you will get insights and ideas from each conversation. You don't have to form a formal "investment club" that invests as a group, although that is something that many do and enjoy. The most important thing is to be reminded that you are not alone, adrift in a sea of obligate consumers, and that what you are doing makes sense to at least one other person.

Become the "leader of your life"

Leadership is often identified as the key ingredient in the fate of clubs, businesses, churches, and nations. The concept is not as often invoked in terms of the lives of individuals, and yet it is just as important. Indeed, more so if you believe that what happens in the world is the sum of actions of individuals.

We recommend that each saver/investor do a personal leadership inventory. This can be seen metaphorically as a tree (Gordon and Berry 2006). Its roots are your core values, the things that guide all aspects of your life. The trunk represents your skills and how you go about things, your style, if you will. The branches and leaves are how you apply your values, skills, and style to the problems and opportunities that arise in your life. Finally, the fruit comprises the relationships you build with others and the accomplishments that give your life scope and meaning.

The leadership inventory is hard to do, if it is to be any good. We don't often think carefully about what we value, but careful thought about this can make it easier to save and invest. For example, if you place a high value on security, you can easily make the connection to the financial security that effective saving and investing will produce. If you place a high value on getting what you want immediately, you have identified something to work on if you are to be successful in deferring consumption in favor of saving. An inventory of your skills may show you some that you are not applying and that could produce more income or pleasure. Many have turned hobbies, from knitting to electronics, into fun plus cash. Your style, how you go about things, may be directly related to how you save and invest. Are you an impulse buyer or investor? Better work on that. Are you overly cautious, always preparing but seldom doing? Better work on that as well. Are you applying your skills to solve your problems and seize opportunities or are you waiting for others to step in and help?

Finally, are you building the relationships you want and need, and solving problems when they arise? If not, embrace change. Find out why you don't have the relationships you want (often because you haven't pursued them) or solve problems as they arise (often because you would rather not think about them) and initiate pursuit and thought.

As many have said before, including us, self-knowledge is the key to many things. Self-knowledge can confer on you the ability to successfully lead your own life, saving and investing included.

CHAPTER 7

Know the Beast: Beware of Politicians, Brokers, and the Media

"Alignment" is a word popular in management consulting circles. Roughly, it means that the goals and rewards sought by different parts of the same organization have to fit together to produce a whole, consistent outcome. When the organization's pieces aren't aligned, trouble follows. You should know, as a savvy saver and investor, with whom your interests are aligned. These tend to be people seeking the same goals you are, often family and friends. It is even more important to know whose goals are not consistent with yours. We list a few of the latter here and discuss why they are out of alignment.

Know Your Broker

Brokers are people who help you invest. They are sources of both knowledge and action. They can advise you on which investments to make, how long to hold them, and when to sell. They also can do things you can't, at least as easily, the most important of which is to trade stocks. The latter is less important now in the age of do-it-yourself trading platforms, but it is good to have help at least at the outset. Both of the authors of this book still have brokers and value them highly. That being said, by the nature of things, your interests and that of your broker's are not necessarily aligned. To quote from our earlier book, *Buy on the Upside*:

The Wall Street Buy Machine plays the Big Bad Wolf to the beginning investor's Little Red Riding Hood by seeming benign and even helpful, while having a concealed desire to eat the contents of your basket.

According to the National Association of Securities Dealers (NASD), in February 2006, there are 657,813 registered securities representatives working in 115,946 offices for 5,114 brokerage firms in the United States. By comparison, the Bureau of Labor Statistics estimated that dentists numbered 152,000, or about one quarter the number of securities professionals. Everyone has (or has had) teeth, but only about half of us invest in stocks. Why are there so many brokers? The answer is simple: to entice you to buy stocks, bonds, mutual funds and other investments.

You see the Wall Street Buy Machine everywhere. For instance, financial programs on TV and radio routinely tout stocks. Brokerage houses promote their lists of favorite stocks to buy. Popular financial magazines publish article after article about hot stocks and what you should buy. Seductive brochures accompany your monthly or quarterly mutual fund or brokerage account statements with the merits of owning stocks. Brokers, trying to earn a living from sales commissions, routinely call you to hawk the latest "great stock" or fund. After you pay for a subscription, a newsletter writer provides lists of stocks you must own now. Stock mutual funds ads tell you how much money you can make in the long run. The federal government gives you tax breaks to maintain a retirement account that presumably contains stocks. And your employer sets up plans so you can buy stocks for your retirement account. The *Machine* tells us to buy stocks at anytime at any price. We retail investors are confronted by a withering campaign of buy, buy, buy.

Wall Street has a "buy machine" because every time a stock is traded, some third party on Wall Street or its equivalent elsewhere makes a fee. Thus, the broker and Wall Street have a vested interest in having you trade stocks. You, on the other hand, should only want to trade when it is in your interest. The best of the experienced "inside" people, such as Burton Malkiel and John Bogle, advise you to trade infrequently, or at least as infrequently as possible.

Another nonalignment with your broker occurs because the broker's reward system is different from yours. Brokers are paid to sell certain mutual funds and stocks, above and beyond their commission. You get paid only if they go up in value or pay dividends. The broker gets paid no matter what the shares subsequently do.

The third big nonalignment comes through mutual fund fees. These vary widely and are not often correlated with fund performance in the market. You, if you buy these funds, pay these fees. Your broker does not and, thus, has little incentive to tell you much about the fees charged by the funds he recommends, although a good broker will do so anyway.

There are two easy remedies for these structural nonalignments with your broker. One is to know about them and consider what they mean in relation to any advice your broker gives you. At least verify any glowing predictions about a particular stock or fund by independent research. You can either do this yourself on the Internet or in the library, or you can invoke the second easy remedy: go to a fee-for-service financial adviser. This person isn't (or shouldn't be) selling anything but advice and so may be more objective. The third remedy for broker nonalignment is harder. It is to become your own advisor/broker. Or at least to make all investment decisions on your own and use your broker to criticize them before buying or selling.

Understand Politicians and the Media

We group politicians and the media because they are similar in their lack of alignment with you as a saver/investor. Yet they are marvelously aligned with each other, although each often portrays the other as an adversary. Politicians have to get reelected on a fairly short time scale; two to four years in this country at most. Newspapers, TV, radio, and increasingly, the Internet live by advertising revenue. This means that they have to be "filled up" with attractive content every day. Thus, the orientation of both politicians and media is relentlessly short term, whereas your length of view as a saver/investor must necessarily be much longer.

This is not the only misalignment between you and politicians and the media, but it is the principal one to watch out for. Politicians and the media are aligned with each other by the need to capture public interest and approval on a short-term, often daily, basis. Thus, they are adept at creating and publicizing ideas and events that do this. What happens in the longer term recedes into insignificance for them, except perhaps as a philosophical pastime. But what happens in the long term determines whether you retire comfortably or with grocery bagging and dog food for a support system. So when you read a news story that tells you that you must (or must not) invest in a given company, don't act, but verify. When a politician tells you what is good for you in a saving and investment sense, don't take it to heart before determining whether it is good for you in the long run, as well as for the politician in the short run. Don't misunderstand. This has nothing to do with political parties or "truth in reporting." There are problems with graft, fraud, and dishonesty in every walk of life, including politics and the media. But we don't mean that. Rather, we want you to understand and act as though their benefit is not necessarily aligned with yours.

Even the media geared directly to the saver/investor isn't completely infallible.

In its July 2005 issue, *Money* magazine spells out the fifty smartest things to do with your money that will help you attain financial security. We reviewed the list and our comments are in italics. The first recommendation is to open a home-equity line of credit (*get yourself into debt for starters*), and the last recommendation is to renovate your kitchen so your house will have more value (*use the home-equity loan to pay for renovations?*). In between, we are told to change the oil in the car; buy regular gas for the car to save money (*buy a fuel-efficient car in the first place*); buy running shoes so you can run instead of paying fees to a gym or health club; dicker with your doctor over medical fees (*you can negotiate fees with some orthopedic surgeon after your knees give out from running*); spend yourself into poverty so your kid can get financial help for college (*say what?*); have your kid open an IRA to save for college (*which way is it, spend or save?*); buy Berkshire Hathaway stock, which is managed by Warren Buffett (*B shares cost only $2,840 a share*); donate stock, not cash, to a charity (*but I just bought stock*); buy inexpensive wine (*have a beer instead?*); start a small home business so you can deduct certain household expenses (*good luck, the IRS wasn't born yesterday*). What were the *Money* people smoking when they drew up this list? We don't know, but be assured that a blanket application of these "tips" is not aligned with your best interest. On the other hand, a few make sense: fund your retirement account to the maximum allowed; save and invest regularly; automate your stock purchases; review your investments at least once a year; buy computer software to track your money; have a financial plan; buy quality stocks and buy low-fee mutual funds.

After studying *Money's* recommendations, we have concluded that you do not need a long to-do list telling you how to spend and save. Rather, follow one overarching commandment that instructs you to spend less and save more. If you simply apply some old-fashioned frugality to both your small and large purchases and save and invest what you would have spent, you will be able to sock away an ever-increasing amount of money for your long-term financial needs. For example, rather than buying the largest car, house, or boat that you think you need, scale back just a bit and invest what you saved by buying smaller. You need not deny yourself the stuff that you want, just cut back a little and invest what you did not spend. Then watch the investments grow over time.

Spend less and save more is a simple yet powerful recipe for building a sound financial future. You can still enjoy your prosperity and live the good life; just do it with a little less stuff and a lot larger nest egg.

CHAPTER 8

Eat Your Spinach: Act Now

Here is our condensed advice. Follow the guidelines below to wealth and happiness by starting to save and invest early in life, or trust your future to luck and an uncaring world.

SAVE and INVEST NOW
Do a budget—Itemize your income and spending. Review your budget every few months.
Save before you spend—Make savings your number 1 priority. Control your spending—Do you really need all that stuff? Pay off credit cards each month—do not accumulate a running balance.
Save as much as possible—Save at least 10 percent of your income, more if possible. Save your salary and wage increases.
Start saving at a young age—Let compound interest work for you. The longer you can accumulate money, the more you will have.
Save regularly and automatically—Put your savings on automatic pilot. Set up automatic transfers from your checking and savings

accounts to your retirement accounts. Keep some cash in a money market account or certificates of deposits.

Set up retirement accounts—Tax shelter your retirement nest egg to increase your returns. Set up automatic transfers from your paycheck into your retirement account. Save the maximum allowed by law. Do not borrow money from your retirement accounts. Use a full-service or discount broker.

ACCUMULATE WEALTH

Buy and hold stocks with safe, increasing dividends—Dividends are cash in your pocket. Avoid very high-yield stocks that could spell trouble.

Reinvest dividends—Accumulate many extra shares over time. It's easy to do—just check the reinvestment box when you buy a stock of fund.

Buy low-fee exchange-traded and index funds—Keep your investment costs to a minimum. Pick from dozens of low-fee funds. *Avoid high-fee managed mutual funds, hedge funds, and annuities*—Keep your investment costs to a minimum. Most managed mutual funds do not beat the market averages. Hedge funds and most annuities are difficult to understand, and they charge very high fees. If you can not explain an investment to a friend in a sentence or two, do not own it.

Don't load up on your employer's stock—Avoid losing your job and your nest egg. Limit your exposure to no more than 10 percent of your portfolio.

Buy Keep cash available to buy bargains—Buy investments when they are cheap. Stock prices routinely fluctuate, so buy when prices are down.

Buy on the price upside—Most upside investments make money. Simple logic tells us that it's easy to make money when prices are rising.

Avoid the price downside—Most downside investments lose money. Let prices fall to a bottom, and then buy an investment when it moves to the upside.

Don't pay too much—Don't chase pricey investments. Avoid price bubbles. If you pay too much, you will have to wait a long time to just beak even. Or you may never make money.

Sell at peaks or bubbles—Sell cyclical investments at their peaks, and sell bubbles before they burst. Do not buy and hold cyclical stocks. Buy and sell a cyclical investment on the upside.

Be skeptical of advice from the "experts"—Brokers, investment analysts, politicians, and the media are not always correct.

Sound Investments at Any Age

Here is a list of appropriate investments for investors with ten or more years to accumulate money. These investments emphasize share accumulation through dividend reinvestment and capital gains from well-established individual stocks.

Long-term Investments
Life Cycle Funds—Buy funds with long durations. Vanguard and Fidelity have low-fee life cycle funds.
Vanguard 500 Index (VFINX)—Low-fee index fund that tracts the S&P 500.
Fidelity Spartan 500 Index Investor (FSMKX)—Low-fee index fund that tracts the S&P 500.
Many other index funds—Funds that tract market indices are appropriate.
Vanguard Equity-Income fund (VEIPX)—Low-fee managed mutual fund that emphasizes dividend-paying stocks.
Market exchange-traded funds—QQQQ and SPY are very popular.
Sector exchange-traded funds—Many ETFs that follow specific industry sectors are available. Some sectors can be very volatile.

International index and exchange-traded funds—Own diversified portfolios of foreign companies. May have high fees.

Individual Stocks from Mergent's Dividend Achievers—These stocks pay safe, increasing dividends and are appropriate to buy and hold.

Companies with strong earning growth—Own these stocks for capital gains and not dividends. Avoid "fad" and "hyped" stocks. *Individual stocks that pay safe, increasing dividends*—Examples include: General Electric, Wrigley's, Emerson Electric, and AquaAmerica.

SPDR Dividend ETF (SDY)—ETF that tracts stocks with long histories of increasing dividends

iShares Dow Jones Select Dividend Index (DVY)—ETF that includes safe, increasing dividends.

ishares Dow Jones US Utilities (IDU)—ETF that tracts the Dow Jones Utilities average, which includes large electric and natural gas utilities.

PowerShares Dividend Achievers™ (PFM)—ETF with over three hundred dividend-paying stocks.

StreetTracks Series Trust Wilshire REIT Index (RWR)—ETF that includes many real estate investment trusts

Electric utilities stocks—select companies that pay safe, increasing dividends.

Cyclical Stocks—buy on the upside and sell at top. Some cyclical stocks include semiconductor equipment, heavy equipment, chemical, paper, and real estate.

Option income funds—These funds sell options to bring in income. They usually have high yields but can be volatile.

Here is a list of appropriate investments for investors with fewer than ten years to accumulate money. Many of these investments emphasize income and safety. Others emphasize capital gains and share accumulation through reinvesting dividends of index, exchange-traded funds, and dividend-paying individual stocks. Many of the long-term investments are included in this list.

Short-term Investments
Certificates of deposit—Safe and flexible, with no surprises. Can ladder CDs with different maturities. Jumbo CDs pay higher rates. Can buy CDs on the Internet.
Money market funds—Safe and flexible, with no surprises. Park money here until you decide what investments to choose.
Life Cycle Funds—Buy funds with short durations. Vanguard and Fidelity have low-fee life cycle funds.
Vanguard 500 Index (VFINX)—Low-fee index fund that tracts the S&P 500.
Fidelity Spartan 500 Index Investor (FSMKX)—Low-fee index fund that tracts the S&P 500.
Many other index funds—Funds that tract most market indices are appropriate.
Vanguard Equity-Income fund (VEIPX)—Low-fee managed mutual fund that emphasizes dividend-paying stocks.

Market exchange-traded funds—QQQQ and SPY are very popular.

Sector exchange-traded funds—Many ETFs that follow specific industry sectors are available. Some sectors can be very volatile.

International index and exchange-traded funds—Own diversified portfolios of foreign companies. May have high fees.

Individual Stocks from Mergent's Dividend Achievers—These stocks pay safe, increasing dividends, and are appropriate to buy and hold.

Companies with strong earning growth—Own these stocks for capital gains and not dividends. Avoid "fad" and "hyped" stocks.

Individual stocks that pay safe, increasing dividends—Examples include General Electric, Wrigley's, Emerson Electric, and AquaAmerica.

SPDR Dividend ETF (SDY)—ETF that tracts stocks with long histories of increasing dividends

iShares Dow Jones Select Dividend Index (DVY)—ETF that includes safe, increasing dividends.

ishares Dow Jones US Utilities (IDU)—ETF that tracts the Dow Jones Utilities average, which includes large electric and natural gas utilities.

PowerShares Dividend Achievers™ (PFM)—ETF with over three hundred dividend-paying stocks.

Electric utilities stocks—Select companies that pay safe, increasing dividends.

See *buyupside.com* for many examples and articles about making money with specific stocks and other investments. In particular, see the **Dividend Book** (it's free) at **buyupside.com** for a comprehensive presentation of dividend-paying investments.

Our parting advice is to put this list, along with the map from chapter 3, on your refrigerator, computer, or cork board and look at it frequently. If you do what they say, you will meet your goals and be happier.

APPENDIX A

The Magic of Compound Interest

With compound interest, you receive interest on interest. So if you hold an investment for a long period, the value of the investment grows very rapidly after a few years. Compound interest works its magic for investors who are able to save and invest for retirement at an early age.

The following chart shows the annual values of a $10,000 initial investment as it grows at an interest rate of 6 percent each year. After fifty years, the $10,000 grows to $184,200.

Value of a $10,000 Investment at 6% Rate of Return

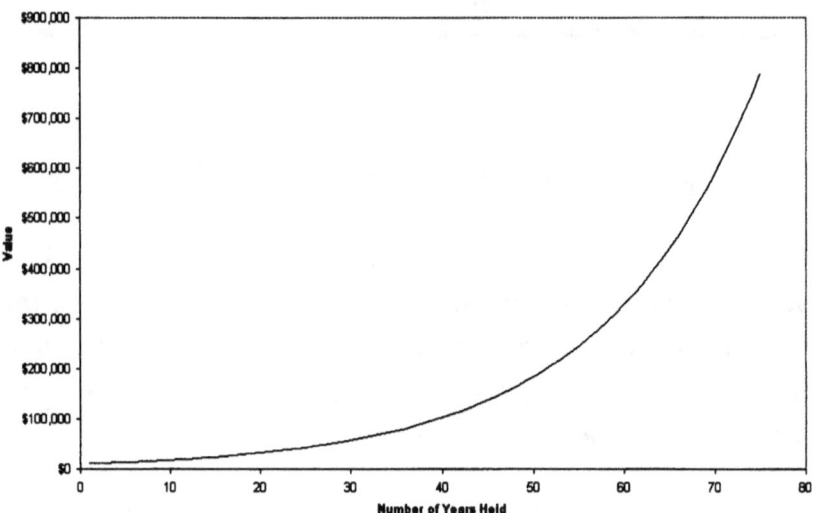

The following table shows the compound interest multipliers for different interest rates and holding periods. For a 6 percent rate of return, each dollar invested grows to $1.34 in five years; $1.79 in ten years; and $3.21 in twenty years. After thirty years the growth accelerates: $1 grows to $10.29 in forty years, and $18.42 in fifty years. So if you invest $10,000 at 6 percent for thirty years, you would have $57,400 ($10,000 x 5.74).

At higher interest rates, the growth after forty and fifty years is very large.

Compound Interest Multipliers					
Year	Rate of Return				
	2%	4%	6%	8%	10%
1	1.02	1.04	1.06	1.08	1.10
2	1.04	1.08	1.12	1.17	1.21
3	1.06	1.12	1.19	1.26	1.33
4	1.08	1.17	1.26	1.36	1.46
5	1.10	1.22	1.34	1.47	1.61
10	1.22	1.48	1.79	2.16	2.59
20	1.49	2.19	3.21	4.66	6.73
30	1.81	3.24	5.74	10.06	17.45
40	2.21	4.80	10.29	21.72	45.26
50	2.69	7.11	18.42	46.90	117.39

The following table shows the effect of compound interest for monthly investments made for many years. Each cell represents the dollars accumulated for a given monthly investment and a given accumulation period. The rate of return is 6 percent, and the accumulation periods are ten, twenty, and thirty years.

For example, if you invest $200 each month at 6 percent for twenty years, you'll have $92,870. If you invest $200 each month at 6 percent for thirty years, you'll have $201,908.

Future Value of Monthly Investments—Six Percent Return			
Monthly Investment	Accumulation Period		
	10 Years	20 Years	30 Years
$50	$8,235	$23,218	$50,477
$100	$16,470	$46,435	$100,954
$200	$32,940	$92,870	$201,908
$300	$49,410	$139,305	$302,861
$400	$65,879	$185,740	$403,815
$500	$82,349	$232,176	$504,769
$1,000	$164,699	$464,351	$1,009,538
$2,000	$329,397	$928,702	$2,019,075

APPENDIX B

The Arithmetic of Saving and Investing

The next three tables show for a specified percent annual rate of return how much money you would need to invest **each month** to attain a given amount of money in a prescribed period. The rates of return are 2 percent, 4 percent, and 6 percent. Use these tables to determine how much money you need to invest each month for a given number of years to achieve your target amount of money for your first year or retirement.

For example, if you have a thirty-year accumulation period, and assume a 2 percent rate of return and want to have $500,000 at the first year of retirement, you must invest $1,015 each month for thirty years. If you have only ten years to accumulate $500,000 at two percent, you must invest $3,767 each month.

For a 6 percent return, the monthly investment amounts decline significantly. You would need to invest $498 each month for thirty years or $3,051 each month for ten years to achieve $500,000. Obviously, it pays to pick higher-yielding investments.

If you start to invest near your retirement, you have to invest a lot of money each month to reach your target. So make every effort to begin your investment program as early as you can.

Monthly Investment Schedule Summary Rate of Return Is 2 Percent			
Initial Balance	Accumulation Period		
	10 Years	20 Years	30 Years
$50,000	$377	$170	$101
$100,000	$753	$339	$203
$200,000	$1,507	$678	$406
$300,000	$2,260	$1,018	$609
$400,000	$3,014	$1,357	$812
$500,000	$3,767	$1,696	$1,015
$1,000,000	$7,535	$3,392	$2,030
$2,000,000	$15,069	$6,784	$4,059

Monthly Investment Schedule Summary Rate of Return Is 4 Percent			
Initial Balance	Accumulation Period		
	10 Years	20 Years	30 Years
$50,000	$340	$136	$72
$100,000	$679	$273	$144
$200,000	$1,358	$545	$288
$300,000	$2,037	$818	$432
$400,000	$2,716	$,1091	$576
$500,000	$3,396	$1,363	$720
$1,000,000	$6,791	$2,726	$1,441
$2,000,000	$13,582	$5,453	$2,882

Monthly Investment Schedule Summary Rate of Return Is 6 Percent			
Initial Balance	Accumulation Period		
	10 Years	20 Years	30 Years
$50,000	$305	$108	$50
$100,000	$610	$215	$100
$200,000	$1,220	$433	$199
$300,000	$1,831	$649	$299
$400,000	$2,441	$866	$398
$500,000	$3,051	$1,082	$498
$1,000,000	$6,102	$2,164	$966
$2,000,000	$12,204	$4,329	$1,991

APPENDIX C

How Long Will Your Money Last?

Suppose you've saved and invested for your retirement and have $100,000 in your retirement account. You decide to start your retirement by withdrawing $5,000 the first year. The next year you take out another $5,000. If you keep taking out $5,000 each year, in twenty years ($100,000/$5,000), you'll be out of money. But if you assume you can add money to the account each year with interest, dividends, and capital gains, you may extend the period to more than twenty years. But what happens if you need to take out more than $5,000, because your expenses increase due to inflation? If you regularly increase the amount of the withdrawal because of inflation, your money may not last the twenty years.

The following chart of drawdown curves shows how much you'll have left in your account after withdrawing money for different number of years. The selected inflation rate is 4 percent, and the different rates of return are 0 percent, 2 percent, 4 percent, 6 percent, 8 percent, and 10 percent. Each year the amount withdrawn increases by 4 percent to keep up with inflation. So eventually the annual withdrawal is large. For example, at 4 percent annual inflation, a $5,000 withdrawal in year 1 grows to $10,534 in year 20, and to $15,593 in year 30.

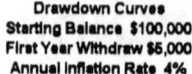

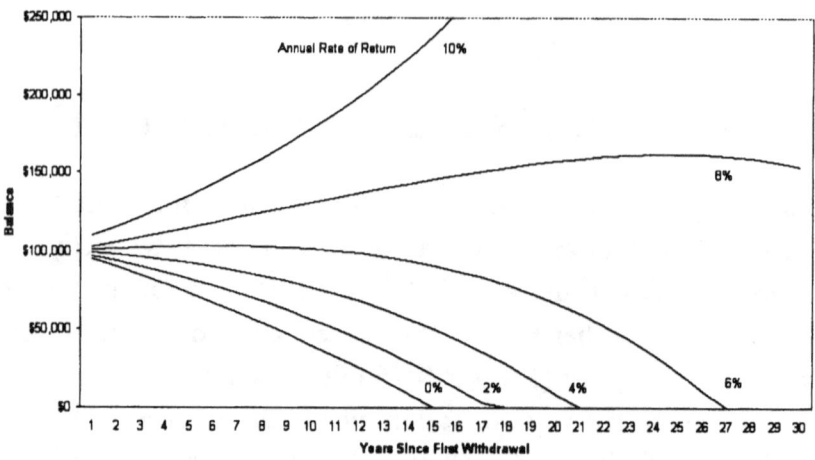

You can see that for 0 percent, 2 percent, 4 percent, and 6 percent
rates of return, you run out of money in 15, 18, 21, and 27 years.
At 8 percent, your account makes money for a few years and
then starts to decline as the inflation-adjusted withdrawals increase.
But you'll have enough money for years and years. For a 10 percent
return, you actually accumulate money in the account even after
inflation and the withdrawals. Why is this? When the rate of return
is high enough, more money is added to the account than is taken
out, so the account balance increases rather than decreases.

But for higher inflation rates, the inflation-adjusted withdrawals
increase so that the account is drained in a few years. For example
at 6 percent, the $5,000 explodes to $15,128 in year 20, and
$27,092 in year 30. At 6 percent inflation, the account goes to a
zero balance in fourteen years for 0 percent, 2 percent, and 4
percent returns. For 6 percent, 8 percent, and 10 percent returns,

the account goes to zero in fifteen years. So at higher inflation rates, even high returns can't protect you.

In the following example, you start with $500,000. Each year you receive a 6 percent return, and the withdrawal amount is adjusted for a 4 percent rate of inflation. The first year withdrawal amounts are: $5,000, $10,000, $15,000, $20,000, or $25,000. The following drawdown curves show the annual balance given different amounts withdrawn each year.

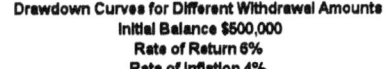

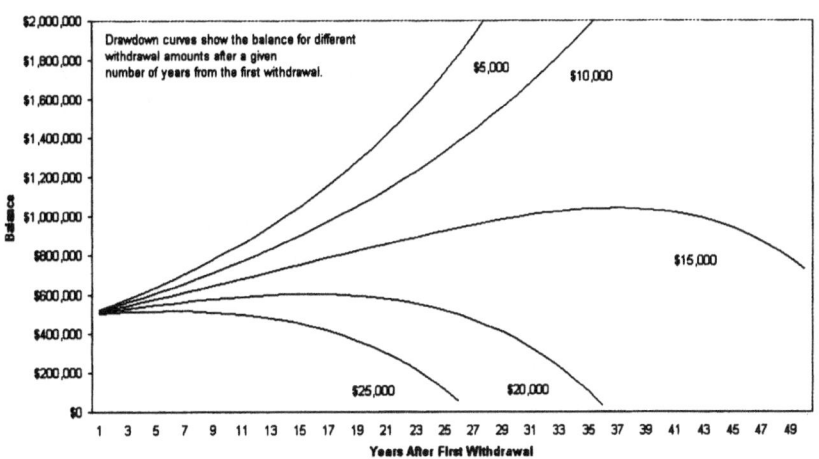

For first-year withdrawals of $5,000 and $10,000, money accumulates in the account, and you never run out. For the $15,000 withdrawal, money accumulates and then starts to decline. For the $20,000 and $25,000 withdrawal amounts, you run out of money in years 37 and 27, respectively, after the first withdrawal.

In real time the annual rates of return and inflation fluctuate. You could have a series of high returns followed by a few years of negative returns, depending on the type of investments in the account. But if the returns consistently outpace inflation, you have a good chance of not running out of money. Obviously, you can't control inflation, but with luck and skill, you might outperform it. On the other hand, if inflation increases significantly and pushes up your expenses and your returns do not keep pace, you could quickly run out of money.

APPENDIX D

buyupside.com Core Stock Portfolio

The **buyupside.com** core stock portfolio is a diversified group of thirty-eight dividend-paying stocks and two exchange-traded funds (ETFs). The portfolio is designed for the long-term buy-and-hold investor who will reinvest dividends.

All the stocks are well-known companies with safe—and in many instances, increasing—dividends. And all the stocks have long-term upside price charts. Most industries in the portfolio are represented by at least two similar stocks.

The two ETFs* are included to have an exposure to technology and Chinese stocks, both of which are volatile but have the promise of long-term growth.

buyupside.com Core Stock Portfolio		
Company	Stock Symbol	Industry
Abbott Laboratories	ABT	Pharmaceuticals
Anheuser-Busch	BUD	Beverages
Aqua America	WTR	Water Utility
Caterpillar	CAT	Heavy Equipment

ChevronTexaco	CVX	Oil and Gas Integrated
Colgate-Palmolive	CL	Personal and Houseware
Deere & Co	DE	Heavy Equipment
Duke Realty	DRE	REIT
EnergySouth	ENSI	Natural Gas Utility
Emerson Electric	EMR	Conglomerate
Exxon Mobil	XOM	Oil and Gas Integrated
Fifth Third Bancorp	FITB	Regional Bank
Florida Public Utilities	FPU	Electric Utility
General Electric	GE	Conglomerate
H. J. Heinz	HNZ	Food
Hershey Foods	HSY	Food
Illinois Toolworks	ITW	Capital Goods
International Paper	IP	Paper and Paper Products
iShares FTSE/Xinhua China 25 Index Fund*	FXI	China
Johnson Controls	JCI	Consumer Cyclical
Johnson & Johnson	JNJ	Pharmaceuticals

Medtronic	MDT	Medical Equipment
3M	MMM	Conglomerate
National City Corp	NCC	Regional Bank
Otter Tail	OTTR	Electric Utility
Peoples Energy	PGL	Natural Gas Utility
PepsiCo	PEP	Beverages and Food
Phelps Dodge	PD	Metal Mining
Piedmont Natural Gas	PNY	Natural Gas Utility
Progress Energy	PGN	Electric Utility
Procter & Gamble	PG	Personal and Houseware
NASDAQ 100 Trust*	QQQQ	Technology
Stryker	SYK	Medical Equipment
Sysco	SYY	Retail (Grocery)
Tootsie Roll Industries	TR	Food
Walgreen	WAG	Retail (Drugs)
Wells Fargo & Co.	WFC	Money Center Bank
WGL Holdings	WGL	Natural Gas Utility
WPS Resources	WPS	Electric Utility
William Wrigley Jr.	WWY	Food (Gum)

APPENDIX E

Upside and Downside Price Patterns

Buy stocks and other investments that are on the price upside. Increasing prices ensure that you will make money. Avoid buying any investment that is on the price downside. No matter how much a stock has fallen in price, it can still decline more.

Upside Price Pattern

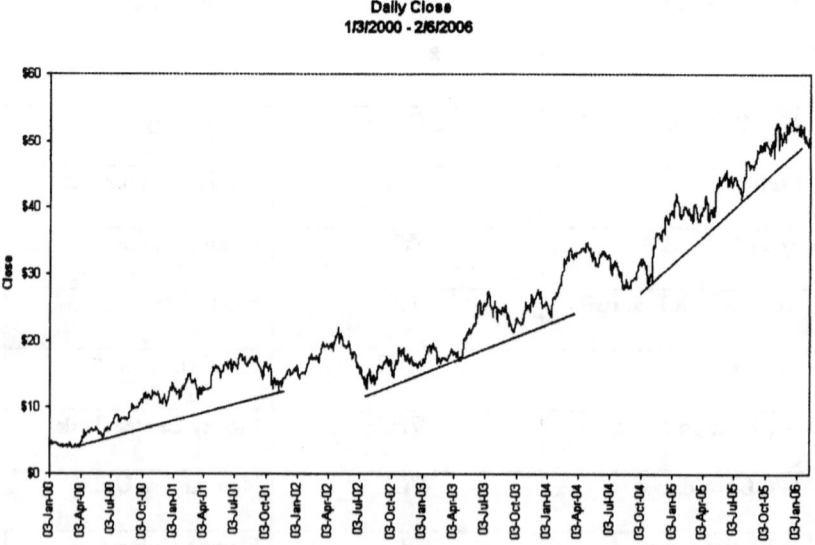

Downside Price Pattern

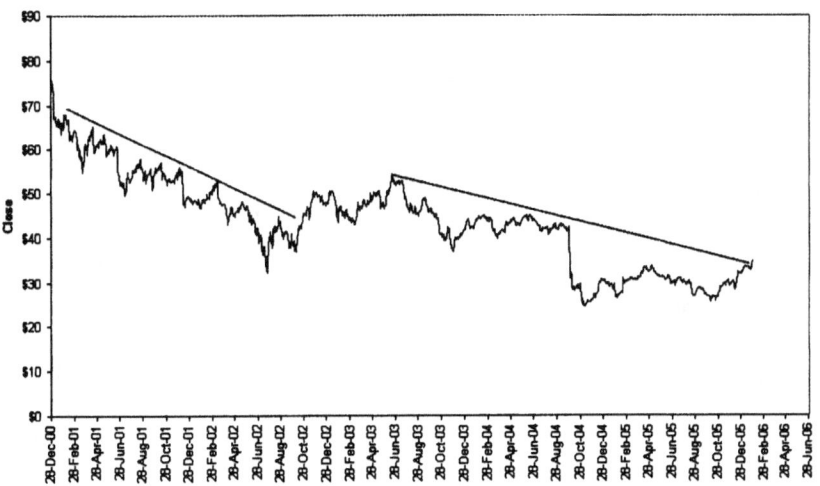

MRK
Daily Close
12/28/2000 - 1/31/2006

www.ingramcontent.com/pod-product-compliance
Lightning Source LLC
Chambersburg PA
CBHW051344170526
45166CB00002B/955